Short Stack Editions | Volume 30

Butter

by Dorie Greenspan

Short Stack Editions

Publisher: Nick Fauchald
Creative Director: Rotem Raffe
Editor: Kaitlyn Goalen
Copy Editor: Abby Tannenbaum
Marketing Manager: Erin Fritch

ISBN 978-0-9986973-0-7

Printed in Virginia
November 2017

Table of Contents

Go-Alongs

Sweets

Well, finally.

Looking back, it seems surprising that butter wasn't one of the very first ingredients we tackled on our Short Stack journey (which began five years ago!) given its ubiquity and importance in both classic and modern cooking (and especially baking). But here we are, 30 editions in—*bon anniversaire!*—and we're just now unwrapping the stick.

Luckily, the wait was worth it, because it created the ultimate alignment: a meditation on this essential ingredient brought to you by one of our essential recipe legends, Dorie Greenspan.

There's a good chance you've cooked (or eaten) a Dorie Greenspan creation without even knowing it. Her recipes are so stalwart and unassumingly delicious that they've reached far and wide through her many award-winning cookbooks, columns for the *New York Times* and *Washington Post* and countless magazine articles.

So it's delightful, though not unexpected, that this edition is a quiver full of butter-rich essentials, each shot straight to the heart of why we love this ingredient so much. Look no further than this little book for staples such as a proper lemon curd and an easy-to-handle béarnaise sauce, both of which exemplify butter's technical role in the kitchen. And as for butter's flavor, a properly over-the-top rich dish like the Robuchon-ish potatoes, modeled after those made by the French chef, is an apt tribute.

All along, we've worked to make cookbooks that are both collectible and utilitarian. What a thrill to reach number 30 and realize that, with the help of our brilliant, talented authors, we've done just that.

Now pass the butter.

—*The Editors*

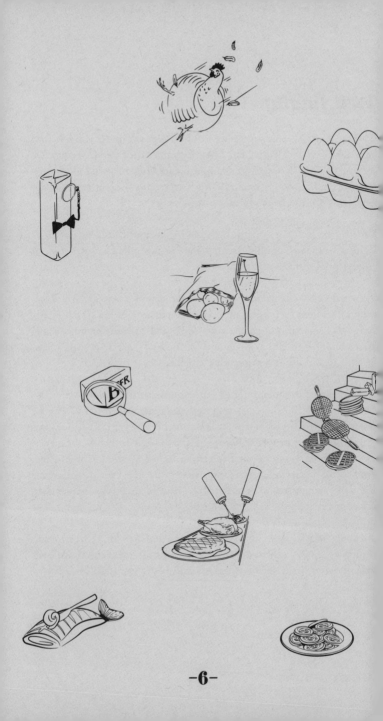

Introduction

I knew I was in the right country when, on an early trip to Paris, a woman I'd only just met suggested I taste the butter. Straight up. No bread. No nothing. She instructed me to taste it for sweetness and for acidity. She knew I was a foreigner, and she wanted me to enjoy my time in her country and to appreciate one of its great culinary treasures. *Merci, Madame.*

Butter is a culinary treasure in countries around the globe and indispensable in our American kitchens. As a baker, I'd be lost without it. Ditto as a cook. Whenever it's used, it adds flavor, texture, structure and often a touch of luxury. Everything we want.

I've told this story before, but it's worth repeating, especially here. Many years ago, I asked the late Lionel Poilâne, the renowned French bread baker, for his recipe for sugar cookies. The cookies were very much like ones my grandmother—and probably thousands of other grandmothers—made (think shortbread). I'd known Poilâne a long time and hadn't thought I was being unreasonable in approaching him. His answer was a quick, "No." But it was the explanation for his refusal that startled me most: "You won't be able to bake these cookies because your butter isn't good enough."

Well, it turned out that my butter was good enough. I brought some all-American butter to Paris, we baked the cookies together and I left with the recipe—and an increased respect for an ingredient I'd always had on hand but hadn't always paid much attention to.

Sometimes you have to go away to return with a new understanding of what you've got. What we've got in America is a steady supply of reliably made butter that allows us to be what many French people aren't: ambitious home bakers and adventurous daily cooks.

The recipes in this edition play with a mix of ideas. Some are homey, some a little exotic. Some are from the American me, some from the Parisian. It's food I cook all the time for my little family and large group of friends.

In some recipes, like the mashed potatoes that are an homage to those made famous by the chef Joël Robuchon, butter is front and center. (I always thought the Robuchon dish should have been called Mashed Butter with Potatoes.) You get the butter in the Lemon Curd, the wonderful scallops, butter-poached in the oven, and the Buttermilk Biscuits, which get their beautiful flaky layers from butter that's rubbed into the dough. In other recipes, the butter is indispensable but not so prominent. It's what holds the Miso-Butter Double-Salmon Rillettes together, gives the Frontier Clam Chowder its body and the onions in the galette their burnished color and deep, sweet, caramel flavor.

Cook and bake through these recipes and you'll come to know all the ways butter enhances our food. As my friend Julia Child used to say, "Butter is better." Of course, she was right.

—Dorie Greenspan

Recipes

Butter Basics

Salted & Sweet Butter

Butter comes either salted or sweet (also called unsalted). Although all salted butter contains some amount of salt (salt used to be added as a preservative, but today it's added primarily for flavor), some salted butters are noticeably salty. The problem is the word *some*. Since the amount of salt can vary from butter to butter, it's best to use unsalted butter in the kitchen and add as much salt as you'd like to each dish. All of these recipes were tested with unsalted butter. If you prefer salted butter, use it—just remember to adjust the salt in each dish.

Cultured Butter

With this kind of butter, the cream is treated with cultures (like yogurt), allowed to ferment and then churned. The result is a fuller flavor with noticeable acidity. It's easier to find cultured American butters these days, but, as with salted butters, not all cultured butters are the same. My favorite, made by Vermont Creamery, has tang and produces a different (and wonderful) sensation on your tongue due to its very high butterfat content. I rarely use this butter in cooking, but I do like it in baking; try it in the Vanilla Butter Cookies (page 40).

European Butter

The standards for the minimum amount of butterfat in butter are different in Europe and America. Abroad, the minimum is 82 percent; here, it's 80 percent; everywhere, it's lower for salted butter. So, whenever you use European butter, you're likely to have a richer dish. When I cook and bake in Paris, I don't make any adjustments in my recipes to make allowances for the difference in butterfat, so if you'd like to try a higher-fat European butter, go for it. It will be particularly good in the Sweet & Savory Butter Crust (page 36) and the Buttermilk Biscuits (page 34). Oh, silly me—it'll be great in everything.

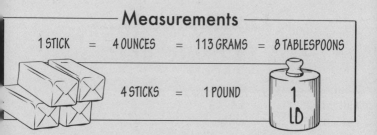

Measurements

1 STICK	=	4 OUNCES	=	113 GRAMS	=	8 TABLESPOONS

4 STICKS = 1 POUND

1 LD

Room-Temperature Butter

Proper room-temperature butter is still slightly cool; it's really more about texture than temperature. The butter should be soft but not squishy. The stick should hold its shape (a little pressure should leave an indentation), and it should be pliable—if you mash it with a spatula, you shouldn't have to fight it.

Storing Butter

Keep butter in the refrigerator, well wrapped and away from foods with strong odors. It can be kept in the freezer for almost forever, but let's call it a year; defrost it overnight in the fridge. Butter can be kept out at cool room temperature for a day, longer in a butter bell or crock. However, my own preference is to store butter in the refrigerator and then pull it out about 20 minutes before I need it.

Clarified Butter

Clarified butter is a magical thing: It's butter without water (you simmer it away) that won't burn when used over high heat. To clarify butter, place the butter in a saucepan, bring it to a simmer and let it bubble gently until it's covered with foam. Don't stop there! Keep simmering the butter until the foam sinks to the bottom and the bubbling just about stops. Line a fine-mesh sieve with cheesecloth or a coffee filter, pour the butter through it into a container, cool and cover. The butter will keep in the fridge for at least 2 months.

Cinnamon-Chile Caramel Corn

Here is popcorn for grown-ups to munch—its edgy, almost bitter caramel is bolstered with cinnamon and harissa. It's also popcorn for grown-ups to make: The caramel—a mixture of brown sugar, honey and lots of butter—bubbles and seethes while it cooks and bubbles and seethes even more when the baking soda goes in. It isn't kid stuff. Pay attention and enjoy the show.

6 cups popped plain popcorn (not buttered or flavored)

½ teaspoon baking soda

½ teaspoon fine sea salt

½ teaspoon cinnamon

½ teaspoon ground harissa or chile powder

1½ sticks (12 tablespoons) unsalted butter, cut into chunks

⅔ cup packed light or dark brown sugar

3 tablespoons honey

serves
·4·

Oil a large bowl with cooking spray and toss in the popcorn.

In a small bowl, whisk together the baking soda, salt, cinnamon and harissa or chile powder.

In a medium saucepan over medium heat, stir together the butter, sugar and honey and bring to a boil. Cook, stirring frequently, for about 5 minutes, until the color is a light mahogany. Remove the mixture from the heat and stir in the baking soda mixture. The caramel will bubble up furiously; stir just as furiously to evenly incorporate everything. Pour the caramel over the popcorn.

Working with two heatproof spatulas, turn the popcorn around for a few minutes. You won't get a perfectly even caramel coating, but you'll come close.

The popcorn is ready to eat as soon as it cools, or it can be crisped in the oven.

To crisp: Preheat the oven to 250°. Using a heatproof spatula, scrape the popcorn onto a parchment- or foil-lined baking sheet and spread it out. Bake for 1 hour, turning every 20 minutes to make sure nothing sticks and everything bakes evenly. Remove the popcorn from the oven and let it cool on the baking sheet.

The popcorn will keep in a paper bag (as long as there's no humidity) or a sealed container at room temperature for a few days.

Butter-Roasted Spiced Almonds

Everyone should have a few house specials, dishes that guests look forward to having when they visit. For me, it's cheese puffs (page 20)—my go-to nibble with aperitifs—and some variation on these spiced nuts. Of course, you can use different nuts (cashews are great here) and play with the spices. In fact, I hope you will, so this truly will be *your* house special. (If you double the recipe, you may want to use two baking sheets.)

½ pound unblanched whole almonds

1 tablespoon unsalted butter

1 tablespoon maple syrup

1 teaspoon light or dark brown sugar

1 teaspoon fleur de sel, plus more for sprinkling

¾ teaspoon garam masala

¾ teaspoon cinnamon

Pinch of cayenne pepper

serves
·4·

Preheat the oven to 350° and place a rack in the center position. Spread the almonds out on a nonstick (or parchment-paper-lined) rimmed baking sheet and roast for 5 minutes.

Meanwhile, put all the other ingredients in a medium saucepan and cook over medium heat, stirring, until the butter melts and the mixture is smooth. Add the warm nuts and cook, stirring often, for 2 to 3 minutes, until the nuts are coated. Return the nuts to the baking sheet, spreading them out in an even layer (they won't bake well if they're in clumps).

Bake for 10 minutes, stirring the nuts after they've roasted for 5 minutes. Transfer the baking sheet to a cooling rack, sprinkle the nuts with more salt, if desired, and cool completely.

The nuts will keep, stored in a tightly sealed container protected from humidity, for up to 1 week. If they get sticky, pop them back into a 350° oven for 5 minutes.

Bread &
Chocolate

This is less a recipe than a way to pretend you're a French kid coming home to a classic after-school treat. The most famous rendition of the bread-and-chocolate combination is the chocolate croissant, but it's often far simpler: just good bread with good butter and good chocolate.

1 large (½-inch-thick) slice country bread

1½ teaspoons unsalted butter, or more to taste

About ¼ cup chopped bittersweet chocolate

Fleur de sel or Maldon flaky salt

serves
-1-

Preheat the broiler. Place the bread on a foil-lined baking sheet about 6 inches from the heat source. Broil until the bread is lightly toasted on both sides. Remove the baking sheet, shut the oven door and turn off the broiler.

Spread the butter over the bread (use more butter if you'd like) and scatter the chopped chocolate on top. Slide the baking sheet back into the still-warm oven and allow the chocolate to melt. You can smooth the chocolate over the bread, if that's your druthers, but I think it's nice when it's a little rougher. Sprinkle with salt and eat *immédiatement*.

Cornmeal Waffles

Without butter, waffles are just dry pancakes. I'm exaggerating only a bit. The batters for waffles and pancakes are similar, but butter plays a bigger role in waffles. It's part of what accounts for waffles' crisp texture, lovely golden color and flavor, of course, but it's also what makes waffles slip off the grids so easily. I sweeten this cornmeal waffle with maple syrup, but if you'd like a more savory waffle, use just 1 to 2 tablespoons of syrup and think about adding some rosemary or cooked bacon. Reheat any leftover waffles in a toaster.

1 cup all-purpose flour

1 cup yellow cornmeal

2 teaspoons baking powder

½ teaspoon baking soda

¼ teaspoon salt

2 cups buttermilk, well shaken

3 tablespoons maple syrup, plus more for serving

2 large eggs

½ stick (4 tablespoons) unsalted butter, melted

makes 6 waffles

Heat your waffle iron according to the manufacturer's directions. (FYI: I use a waffle iron that makes 6½-inch rounds.)

In a large bowl, whisk together the flour, cornmeal, baking powder, baking soda and salt. In a second bowl, whisk together the buttermilk, maple syrup and eggs. Pour the liquid ingredients over the dry and whisk gently. When the mixture is almost combined, stir in the butter.

Spray or lightly butter the grids of your iron. For each waffle, spread ½ cup of batter (or less, depending on your iron) across the grids. Close the lid and cook until browned and crisp. Drizzle with maple syrup and serve hot.

Note: If you'd like, you can keep finished waffles warm in a 200° oven while you make the rest of the batch.

Coddled Eggs & Buttered Soldiers

These make a luxurious breakfast or brunch dish, but I love them as an appetizer. Coddled eggs, not your usual opener, are simple and elegant. And dipping the buttered bread into the soft eggs is both a little messy and a lot of fun.

2 tablespoons minced parsley or chives, divided

1 tablespoon unsalted butter, plus more for the ramekins or cups

8 scallions, trimmed and cut into 1-inch-thick slices

Fine sea salt and freshly ground black pepper

4 large organic eggs, at room temperature

4 teaspoons heavy cream

4 thin slices smoked salmon, for serving

4 generously buttered toast fingers (soldiers), for serving

serves
·4·

Set up your steamer by placing a steaming rack with a flat bottom inside a large pot. The steaming rack should be flat and large enough to rest 4 heatproof ramekins or cups on it (or stack them like a pyramid). Add enough water to the pot so that it will come 2 inches below the rack. With the steaming rack in place, bring the water to a simmer.

Grease four 4- to 6-ounce heatproof ramekins or cups. Lightly sprinkle with some of the herbs.

In a small skillet, melt the tablespoon of butter and add the scallions; season with salt and pepper and cook until the scallions are almost tender, 2 to 3 minutes; stir in half of the remaining herbs.

Divide the scallions among the ramekins, then crack an egg into each ramekin, season with salt and pepper and drizzle 1 teaspoon of cream into each ramekin.

Place the eggs in the steamer, cover and cook for 5 to 7 minutes, until the whites are set and yolks still runny. Remove the eggs from the steamer and sprinkle with the last of the herbs.

Place a strip of smoked salmon on each piece of buttered toast and serve, encouraging everyone to dunk the soldiers into the eggs.

Cheese Puffs, aka Gougères

I'm too much of a tinkerer to ever let anything stay the same for long, and so it is with these cheese puffs. The core recipe—based on the French dough pâte à choux—stays, but I'm always playing with the cheeses, the accent spices and the occasional additions. Here, the recipe gets a mix of regular and smoked cheese, which makes it just as good with beer as with my usual serve-along, Champagne.

½ cup milk

1 stick (8 tablespoons) unsalted butter

1 teaspoon salt

1 cup all-purpose flour

5 large eggs, lightly beaten

4 ounces shredded sharp cheddar cheese

2 ounces shredded smoked cheddar, Gouda or Jack cheese

makes 36

Preheat the oven to 425° and position the racks in the upper and lower thirds. Line two baking sheets with parchment paper.

In a medium saucepan, bring the milk, ½ cup of water, the butter and salt to a boil. Add the flour all at once, lower the heat and stir vigorously for 3 to 4 minutes, or until the flour has been absorbed, the dough forms a ball and there's a thin film on the bottom of the pan. Scrape the dough into a stand mixer bowl (or a bowl you can use with a mixer). Beat the dough at medium speed for 2 minutes and then, still beating, gradually add the eggs. The mixture may separate, but after you've added the eggs and beaten the mixture for an extra minute or two, the dough will be smooth and satiny. Turn the mixer to low and beat in both cheeses.

Using a medium scoop (1½ tablespoons) or a spoon, portion the dough into mounds and place on the baking sheets about 2 inches apart. Slide the baking sheets into the oven and immediately turn the temperature down to 375°.

Bake for 20 to 30 minutes, rotating the sheets between upper and lower racks and from front to back after 15 minutes, or until the puffs are golden, firm to the touch and puffed … natch. Serve immediately.

Miso-Butter
Double-Salmon Rillettes

Rillettes, so very French, are usually made with pork cooked in its own fat until it's as spreadable as jam. These are lighter, made with both fresh and smoked salmon and miso butter. The butter gives the rillettes their luxurious texture (it also holds everything together), and the miso is the flavor that few people can identify on first bite. Serve the rillettes on toast or crackers with white or sparkling wine. Cocktail hour perfection.

1 lemon

¼ cup white wine

Fine sea salt and freshly ground black pepper

8 ounces skinless salmon fillets, cut into small cubes

3 tablespoons unsalted butter, softened

3 tablespoons white or yellow miso

1 small shallot, minced

4 ounces finely chopped smoked salmon

3 tablespoons mixed herbs or cilantro, minced

Sriracha

Toast or crackers, for serving

serves
6

Cut 3 thin strips of lemon peel and toss them into a small saucepan along with the wine, ¼ cup of water and a pinch of salt; bring to a boil. Add the fresh salmon, lower the heat, cover and cook for just 1 minute. Remove the pan from the heat, keep covered and let rest for 10 minutes. Strain the salmon, discarding the liquid and peel, and chill for about 20 minutes (or for up to 1 day).

In a mixing bowl, beat the butter with a flexible spatula until it's spreadable. Mix in the miso. Finely grate the lemon's remaining zest and add it to the bowl along with the juice from half the lemon. Add the shallot, a pinch of salt and a little pepper. Blend thoroughly, then stir in both salmons, the herbs and a squirt of Sriracha. Taste and season with more salt, pepper and Sriracha, if desired.

Transfer the rillettes to the refrigerator. The rillettes are best after they've been refrigerated for 6 hours, but they're fine once the butter is chilled. Serve with toast or crackers. The rillettes will keep, covered and refrigerated, for up to 3 days.

Pressed & Griddled Cheese Sandwich

A carefully made grilled cheese sandwich is a gustatory wonder. Its key ingredients are bread that's firm enough to hold its own against heat and pressure but soft enough to produce a tender sandwich; full-flavored, high-quality cheese (my preference is Comté or an aged cheddar), cut about ⅛ inch thick; and clarified butter. The butter flavors the bread and allows it to color deeply without becoming too dark or, worse, burnt. Make the sandwich on a griddle or in a heavy skillet and use another heavy skillet to press it down. The greater the pressure, the more the ingredients will blend and the better your sandwich will be.

2 slices whole-grain sandwich bread

About 2 teaspoons mayonnaise

2 slices aged cheese, such as Comté or cheddar

1 thick slice tomato (optional)

2 slices crisp-cooked bacon (optional)

1 to 2 tablespoons clarified butter (page 11), at room temperature

makes
-1-

Spread one side of a slice of bread with some mayonnaise, top with a slice of cheese, tomato and bacon (if using) and another slice of cheese. Spread mayo on the other slice of bread and close the sandwich.

Place a griddle or heavy skillet over medium heat. Brush the cooking surface lightly with clarified butter, then brush both sides of the sandwich with the butter. Lay the sandwich in the pan, weight with a(nother) heavy skillet (or a plate with a couple of cans of beans on top to weigh it down) and cook until the underside of the sandwich is beautifully golden. Flip, weight and cook until the top of the sandwich is golden and the cheese is hot and bubbling. Serve without a second's hesitation.

Frontier Clam Chowder

Where I live in Connecticut, clam chowder is rich and creamy. But across the border, in Rhode Island, it's thin and brothy. My own chowder is a combination of the two styles. It's thickened with a mix of butter and flour and cooked with a blend of clam juice, milk and cream. It's not as Spartan as my Rhode Island neighbors' soup, but neither is it as rich as it seems. Soup diplomacy.

3 tablespoons unsalted butter

¼ cup diced pancetta

1 large sweet onion, finely chopped

2 stalks celery, finely sliced

1 garlic clove, minced

2 sprigs thyme

1 bay leaf

Salt and freshly ground black pepper

serves ·4·

¼ cup all-purpose flour

¼ cup white wine

2 cups clam juice

¾ pound Yukon Gold potatoes, peeled and cut into small cubes

1 cup whole milk

1 cup heavy cream

About 12 ounces chopped clams (raw or canned)

Oyster crackers, for serving

In a large pot, combine the butter, pancetta, onion, celery, garlic, thyme and bay leaf, season lightly with salt and pepper and cook over low heat, stirring occasionally, until the vegetables soften, about 10 minutes. Sprinkle with the flour and cook, stirring, for 2 minutes. Add the wine, increase the heat and cook until it evaporates. Pour in 1 cup of water and the clam juice, add the potatoes and bring to a boil. Lower the heat and cook, uncovered, until the potatoes are tender, about 15 minutes. Pour in the milk and cream and gently simmer for 4 minutes—don't boil! Stir in the clams, taste for salt and pepper and cook just until the clams are warmed through (or cooked, if they were raw). Divide the chowder among four soup bowls and serve with oyster crackers, of course.

Béarnaise Sauce & Grilled Steak

Béarnaise is the classic French sauce served with steak. Like its sister hollandaise, it's an emulsion of egg yolks and butter (try to imagine warm mayonnaise). Its distinguishing characteristics are its ultra-creamy consistency, its appealing note of acidity and the foundational flavor of tarragon. Although the sauce has a reputation for being tricky, it's a cinch to make in a blender. One caution: The eggs are not fully cooked, so make certain to use the freshest organic eggs you can. And while I'm suggesting the traditional go-along, a pan-seared steak, the sauce is also extra good drizzled over steamed vegetables.

2 tablespoons white wine vinegar, plus more to taste

2 tablespoons white wine

1 tablespoon plus 1½ teaspoons minced tarragon, divided

½ shallot, finely minced

Salt and freshly ground black pepper

1 stick (8 tablespoons) unsalted butter

3 large organic egg yolks

4 cooked filets mignons or other steaks

serves ·4·

In a small saucepan, add the vinegar, wine, 1 tablespoon of tarragon, the shallot and a pinch each of salt and pepper and cook until the mixture is reduced to 2 tablespoons. Hawkeye it: Once it starts reducing, it can disappear quickly.

In another saucepan over medium heat, melt the butter without letting it come to a boil.

Drop the eggs into a blender, turn the machine to high and, with the blades whirring, very slowly drizzle in the warm, melted butter. Go really slowly, stopping once to scrape down the jar. When all the butter has been added, keep the blender on high and drizzle in the reduced herb-vinegar mixture. Taste the sauce for salt and pepper, add the remaining 1½ teaspoons of tarragon and, if you think it needs it, a splash more vinegar. Stir to blend or do this with the machine. You'll have about ⅔ cup of sauce.

The sauce is ready to use immediately, or you can serve it at room temperature. You can also pour it into a thermos to keep it warm; use it within an hour. Serve alongside or on top of the steaks.

Spatchcocked Butterball Chicken

"Spatchcocked chicken" is fun to say, more fun to eat. Spatch-cocking involves removing the bird's backbone, pressing down on the breastbone to flatten the chicken and then patting yourself on the back for a job well done. Here, you slip softened herb butter under the bird's skin so that it self-bastes, like Butterballs of yore. The prep is (literally) hands-on, but the roasting is hands-off and it turns out an especially juicy and flavorful bird in about an hour.

2 tablespoons chopped fresh tarragon, plus 3 sprigs

Finely grated zest of 1 lemon

½ stick (4 tablespoons) unsalted butter, softened

Fine sea salt and freshly ground black pepper

One 4-pound chicken, preferably organic, patted dry

1 unpeeled head garlic, cut in half across the equator

1 small yellow onion, quartered

3 sprigs thyme

¾ cup chicken stock

¼ cup dry white wine

Country bread (optional), for serving

serves
·4·

Preheat the oven to 425°. Choose a skillet or roasting pan that will hold the chicken snuggly and be tall enough to hold the stock and wine too.

In a bowl, combine the chopped tarragon, lemon zest and butter, season with ½ teaspoon of salt and ¼ teaspoon of pepper and mash with a fork to blend.

To spatchcock the chicken, set it on a cutting board and, using shears or a cleaver, separate the backbone from the ribs (save the backbone for

your next batch of chicken stock). Turn the chicken breast side up, place both your hands in the center of the breastplate and press down hard until you hear the breastbone snap (you'll need to use some force); the chicken should be flattened at this point.

Carefully work your fingers under the skin, loosening it from the meat all over the chicken. Now work three-quarters of the butter under the skin. Don't worry about getting an even layer; once you've got dabs of butter underneath, you can massage the skin to smooth them out. Rub the remaining butter over the outside of the chicken.

In the center of a roasting pan, arrange the garlic, onion and sprigs of tarragon and thyme and season with salt and pepper. Place the chicken on top of the vegetables and pour the stock and wine around it.

Roast for 45 to 60 minutes, or until the chicken is golden brown and the thigh juices run clear. Cut the chicken into quarters and urge everyone to spread the softened garlic over country bread (if using). If you'd like, you can pour the cooking juices through a fine-mesh sieve and strain into a pitcher to pass around for serving, or you can offer the juices in their natural state, complete with bits of onion and thyme.

Meunière-Style Flounder

Here's a beloved French classic: fish fillets dredged in flour (*meunière* means miller's wife) and cooked in butter that browns in the pan and takes on the toasty flavor of hazelnuts. To brown the butter without burning it, toss in a few bits of cold butter as the fish cooks. If your skillet is small—or your fillets large—cook the fillets in batches. Four tablespoons of butter should be enough for everything, but have a tablespoon or so more at hand, just in case.

⅓ cup all-purpose flour

Fine sea salt and freshly ground black pepper

4 flounder fillets, each 6 to 8 ounces (more fillets if very small), patted dry

About ½ stick (4 tablespoons) cold unsalted butter, divided

1 lemon, cut into quarters

Minced parsley, for garnish

serves ·4·

Put the flour on a plate, season with salt and pepper and dredge the fish in the flour, covering both sides. Tap off excess flour.

Set a large skillet, preferably nonstick, over medium heat and drop in 1½ tablespoons of butter. When the butter melts and the bubbles calm down, slip in as many fillets as you can comfortably fit in a single layer. Reduce the heat to medium low and cook for about 3 minutes, until the flour is golden and the fish is cooked halfway through; the butter will be a nutty brown. Carefully flip the fish over and cook, adding another ½ to 1 tablespoon of butter in small pieces to the pan and spooning the brown butter over the fillets as they cook, another 2 minutes. Repeat, if you've got more fillets.

Squeeze the juice of one-quarter of a lemon over each plate, sprinkle with parsley and serve.

Butter-Poached Scallops in a Pouch

Cooking in a parchment-paper pouch is a traditional way to quickly infuse flavor into delicate seafood. Here, the flavor is butter and lemon, a classic with almost anything that swims, and the seafood is scallops. The twist is the lemon: It's salt-preserved, *citron confit*, a staple in Mediterranean cuisines. You can make and refrigerate the packets up to 6 hours ahead; let them come to room temperature on the counter while you preheat the oven.

Handful of baby spinach

Salt and freshly ground black pepper

4 teaspoons finely chopped preserved lemon, rind only, rinsed and dried

¾ stick (6 tablespoons) unsalted butter, divided

16 sea scallops, preferably all a similar size, patted dry

16 grape or cherry tomatoes, halved

4 tablespoons dry white wine

serves ·4·

Preheat the oven to 475° and place a rack in the center position. Cut four 15-inch squares of parchment paper.

Assemble each pouch: Place a few spinach leaves in the center of the paper, season lightly with salt and pepper (but go easy—the lemon is salty), add ½ teaspoon of lemon and scatter with ½ tablespoon of butter cut into bits. Arrange 4 scallops over the butter, top with another ½ teaspoon of lemon and 8 tomato halves; season lightly with salt and pepper. Add 1 tablespoon of wine and finish with 1 tablespoon of butter cut into bits. Pull up the corners of the parchment to encase the ingredients in a hobo sack and tie with kitchen twine. Place the pouches on a baking sheet.

Cook the pouches for 8 minutes. Place each pouch in a soup bowl. Untie the packets, being careful of the steam, and serve immediately.

Robuchon-ish Potatoes

The Michelin multi-starred French chef Joël Robuchon is famous for his mashed potatoes, which are fabulously delicious and rich beyond rich—they're almost an equal-parts potato-butter emulsion. Buy Yukon Gold potatoes for this and find a partner to work with; you'll need to stir the pot energetically for about 30 minutes. Whatever you do, don't try to speed up the process—too much heat will cause the butter to separate from the potatoes. All is lost at that point. This is a dish that rewards patience.

1 pound Yukon Gold potatoes, scrubbed (don't peel)

2 sticks (16 tablespoons) very cold unsalted butter, cut into 12 pieces each

2 tablespoons whole milk, warmed

Fine sea salt

Freshly ground pepper, preferably white

serves 4 to 6

Put the potatoes in a large pot filled with salted cold water and bring to a boil. Cook the potatoes until they can be pierced easily with a knife, 40 to 60 minutes, depending on their size. Drain well and let cool slightly. When the potatoes are cool enough to handle, slip off the skins. Work the potatoes through a food mill or ricer (not a masher or mixer) and place in a medium-size saucepan.

Place the pan over medium-low heat and cook, stirring constantly, for 3 minutes, until the potatoes are no longer steaming (they may leave film on the bottom of the pan). Reduce the heat to low. Working with wooden spoon, elbow grease and patience, stir the cold butter into the potatoes piece by piece. Keeping the butter cold and adding it slowly is the key to creating an emulsion—if the butter is warm or added too quickly, it will melt into the potatoes rather than bind the mixture

Add another piece of butter only when the last one is almost absorbed. If necessary, move the pan on and off the heat to maintain the right temperature. When all of the butter is in, stir in the milk. Season with salt and pepper and serve immediately.

Butter-Glazed Turnips

I love this technique for cooking and lightly glazing vegetables all at once. And I particularly like it with turnips, a vegetable with a big personality that can always use a little tamping down and a touch of sweetness, both of which it gets here. The turnips are cut into small pieces, cooked with butter and sugar and then finished with a spoonful of honey. The glaze is light, but it's transformative.

2 tablespoons unsalted butter

2 teaspoons sugar

½ teaspoon fine sea salt

1 pound purple-top turnips—
trimmed, peeled and cut into
2-inch cubes

1 teaspoon honey

Freshly ground black pepper

serves **4**

In a medium to large skillet over medium heat, combine the butter, sugar, salt and ¼ cup of water and cook until the sugar and salt have dissolved. Add the turnips, mix to coat them with the liquid, cover the pan and cook at medium low until the turnips are not quite tender, about 8 minutes, mixing occasionally and checking that there's enough water in the pan to bubble around the turnips; add more water, if needed. Remove the cover, turn up the heat a tad higher and finish cooking the turnips. Don't flip them too often—you want to get a little color here and there. When the turnips are cooked through but still al dente, drizzle with the honey, then stir for a minute. Season with pepper, taste for seasoning and adjust as needed. Serve immediately.

Buttermilk Biscuits

This biscuit is for just about any time of day and perfect as a tag-along with just about any kind of meal. It can even be dessert; just add another 2 teaspoons of sugar and use it as the base for strawberry shortcake. Make sure the butter is really cold, and don't overdo it when you work it into the dough. Aim for a rocky-road-like mix; it's the chunks of butter that produce the steam needed to make the biscuits tall and flaky.

2 cups all-purpose flour, plus more for dusting

1 tablespoon baking powder

¼ teaspoon baking soda

1 teaspoon sugar

½ teaspoon fine sea salt

¾ stick (6 tablespoons) cold unsalted butter, cut into 12 pieces

¾ cup cold buttermilk

makes 10 to 12

Preheat the oven to 425° and place a rack in the center position. Have at hand a 2-inch-diameter biscuit cutter (or, in a pinch, a straight-edged glass) and a baking sheet lined with parchment paper or a silicone baking mat.

In a mixing bowl, whisk the dry ingredients together. Add the butter and toss to coat. Working quickly with your fingertips or a pastry blender, cut and rub the butter into the flour until the mixture is pebbly.

Pour in the buttermilk and use a fork to gently toss the ingredients until you have a nice, soft dough. Now, quickly and gently knead the dough, folding it about eight times.

Turn the dough onto a flour-dusted surface, lightly dust the top of the dough with more flour and pat it out until it's ½ inch high. Don't worry too much about accuracy—a light touch is more important.

Cut out as many biscuits as close to one another as you can; transfer them to the baking sheet. Gather the scraps, pat out to ½ inch high and cut more biscuits.

Bake 14 to 18 minutes, or until the biscuits are tall, puffed and golden. Serve immediately unless you plan to sandwich the biscuits with something or turn them into shortcakes; if so, transfer the biscuits to a rack and let them cool. The biscuits can be stored in an airtight container (though they're really best just out of the oven).

Butter-Browned Onion Galette

Onions are chameleons: Eat them raw and they're like apples; cook them lightly and they soften and sweeten; cook them for a long time in butter and they turn darker and sweeter still, and as they caramelize, the butter takes on a nutlike flavor. They're a marvel in this rustic open-faced galette, the French version of a crostata, which you could finish off with some lightly dressed arugula. Keep these caramelized onions in mind for other dishes. They're great as a topping for a burger, layered into a grilled cheese sandwich and served as a bed for mashed potatoes or grilled meat.

½ stick (4 tablespoons) unsalted butter

2 large Vidalia onions—peeled, halved and thinly sliced

3 garlic cloves, minced

1 teaspoon fine sea salt

1 teaspoon sugar

3 rosemary sprigs

Freshly ground black pepper

3 tablespoons grated Parmesan cheese

1 Sweet & Savory Butter Crust (page 36), rolled out

Parmesan shards

serves 6

In a large skillet over medium heat, melt the butter. Add the onions and garlic and cook, stirring, for 10 minutes. Turn the heat to low, stir in the salt, sugar and rosemary and cook, stirring often, until the onions color deeply, about 40 minutes. Don't rush it! Season with pepper and remove the rosemary sprigs. Remove from the heat, set the skillet aside to cool and stir in the grated Parmesan.

Preheat the oven to 400°. Lay the crust out on a parchment-paper- or silicone-mat-lined baking sheet. Spread the onions over the crust leaving a 2-inch border. Gently lift the border up and fold it over the onions. If the dough is too cold and cracks, wait a few minutes. The dough will pleat and be uneven, and that's just what you want.

Bake for 35 to 45 minutes, or until the crust and onions are toasty brown. Place the galette on a rack and let it cool for 10 minutes before scattering the Parmesan shards over the top. Cut the galette with a pizza wheel and serve.

Sweet & Savory Butter Crust

Use this dough for any kind of tart or quiche or even galettes—and any time a recipe calls for pâte brisée. It's truly an all-purpose and truly delicious crust. Bake it to a good golden brown so that you can really appreciate the caramel and nut flavors that are the hallmark of an all-butter crust.

1¼ cups all-purpose flour

1 teaspoon sugar

½ teaspoon salt

¾ stick (6 tablespoons) very cold unsalted butter, cut into bits

1 large egg

1 teaspoon ice water

Makes

one 9 IN. *tart*

– or –

1 *galette*

In a food processor, pulse the flour, sugar and salt. Scatter over the bits of butter and pulse until they're coarsely chopped into the mix. In a small bowl, beat the egg and water together, add the mixture to the machine in three parts and pulse after each one. You want a moist dough that holds together when it's pinched. Turn the dough onto a counter, flatten into a disk and place between sheets of parchment or wax paper.

To make a tart crust: Roll out the dough and fit it into a tart pan. Chill (or freeze) the dough for at least 1 hour before baking.

Preheat the oven to 400°. Press a piece of buttered foil on top of the crust and fill with dry rice or beans. Place the pan on a baking sheet lined with parchment paper or a silicone baking mat. Bake for 20 minutes, remove the foil and weights and bake for another 10 minutes, or until golden. Transfer the baking sheet to a rack and let the crust cool to room temperature.

To make a galette: Roll the freshly made dough into an 11-inch circle and refrigerate (or freeze) it for at least 1 hour before using. Proceed with the directions for making the Butter-Browned Onion Galette (page 35).

Financiers

What makes these small almond cakes fabulously delicious and as rich as their namesake (*financier* means "banker" in French) is butter, lots of it. These are classic French pastries that I like to make in very American mini-muffin tins. If you'd like to make them taste even more Gallic, brown the butter before you add it to the mixture.

1 cup sugar

1 cup almond flour

6 large egg whites

⅔ cup all-purpose flour, plus more for dusting

1½ sticks (12 tablespoons) unsalted butter, melted and warm, plus additional softened butter for the pan

makes **18**

In a medium saucepan, stir the sugar and almond flour together. Mix in the egg whites and place the pan over low heat. Staying glued to the stove and stirring constantly, cook for about 2 minutes, until the mixture is slightly white, runny and hot to the touch. Remove the pan from the heat and stir in the all-purpose flour; gradually blend in the melted butter.

You can cover and chill the batter for up to 3 days or bake it right away.

Preheat the oven to 400° and place a rack in the center position. Generously butter the insides of 18 mini-muffin tins, dust with flour and tap out the excess. Place the tins on a baking sheet. Fill each indentation almost to the top with batter.

Bake the financiers for 11 to 14 minutes, or until the cakes are golden, springy and start to pull away from the sides of the pan. Unmold immediately and serve slightly warm or at room temperature.

French Chocolate Tart

Chapeaus off to whoever invented ganache, the richest expression of chocolate's goodness. Basic ganache comprises three ingredients—cream, chocolate and butter—which combine to form an emulsion. Think silky pudding with a French twist. That it's easy to make is the bonus. Prepare the crust ahead, take 10 minutes to make the ganache and then tuck the dessert away in the fridge until you need it.

1 cup heavy cream

8 ounces semi- or bittersweet chocolate, very finely chopped

½ stick (4 tablespoons) unsalted butter, at room temperature and cut into small pieces

Fully baked Sweet & Savory Butter Crust (page 36), in a tart pan

Lightly sweetened whipped cream

Chocolate shavings, for decoration (optional)

serves
·10·

In a small saucepan over low heat, cook the cream and chocolate, stirring, until the chocolate melts and the mixture smoothens, about 5 minutes. Keep the heat low—don't let it bubble! Turn off the heat, leave the pan on the burner and, bit by bit, add the butter, stirring until the butter melts. When all the butter is in, you should have a velvety, lightly shiny ganache. Pour it into the crust.

Carefully slide the tart into the refrigerator and chill until the chocolate is firm, about 3 hours (you can refrigerate the tart overnight, if you do, cover it with plastic wrap).

When you're ready to serve the tart, top it with whipped cream and chocolate shavings (if using).

Vanilla Butter Cookies

Every baker should have one wonderfully good butter cookie recipe she can rely on, and this is it. The cookie has shortbread's melt-in-your-mouth tenderness, French sablé's crumbliness and a surprising amount of salt—more than usual and just enough to encourage you to keep nibbling (salt can do that). If you can find high-butterfat European-style butter, grab it. If you can get cultured butter for these, so much the better.

2 sticks (16 tablespoons) unsalted butter, at room temperature

½ cup granulated sugar

¼ cup confectioners' sugar, sifted

½ teaspoon salt, preferably sea salt

2 large egg yolks, at room temperature

2 teaspoons pure vanilla extract

2 cups all-purpose flour

Working with a stand or hand mixer on medium speed, beat the butter both sugars and the salt until smooth and very creamy. Reduce the mixer speed to low and beat in the egg yolks, then the vanilla. Turn off the mixer, add the flour all at once and pulse the mixer on low speed to begin incorporating it. When most of the flour has been incorporated continue to mix on low until the flour is blended in and the dough is soft, moist and clumpy—it won't be truly smooth.

Divide the dough in half and shape each piece into a 9-inch-long log Wrap the log in plastic wrap and chill for at least 3 hours (or for up to 3 days; you can freeze the dough for up to 2 months).

Preheat the oven to 350° and place a rack in the center position. Line two baking sheets with parchment paper.

Working with one log at a time, trim the ends off, then slice into ⅓-inch-thick cookies. Arrange them on the baking sheets, leaving an inch between each cookie.

Bake the cookies, one sheet at a time, for 17 to 20 minutes, rotating the baking sheet from front to back at the halfway point. The cookies should be light brown on the bottom, lightly golden around the edges and pale on top. Leave them on the baking sheet for 3 minutes, then carefully transfer them to a rack to cool to room temperature.

The cookies will keep in a tightly sealed container for about 5 days at room temperature; if they're stored in an airtight container, they can be frozen for up to 2 months.

Pear-Cranberry Crisp

This is an almost-classic topping for an almost-classic combination of pears, cranberries and ginger—and yes, it's perfect for Thanksgiving. The topping has an equal amount of flour and oats, making it both crunchy and chewy. Don't skimp on the salt, and make sure the butter is cold; if the butter is warm, you won't get the nubbins and chunklets that make the texture of the topping so good.

For the topping:

1 cup all-purpose flour

1 cup old-fashioned oats

¼ cup light brown sugar

2 tablespoons granulated sugar

¾ teaspoon fine sea salt

1 stick (8 tablespoons) very cold unsalted butter, cut into small pieces

1 teaspoon pure vanilla extract

For the filling:

2 pounds pears—peeled, cored and cut into chunks

½ cup cranberries, fresh or frozen (not thawed)

½ cup sugar

1 teaspoon finely grated ginger

Grated zest and juice of 1 lime

serves
·6·

Make the topping: In a large bowl, mix the flour, oats, both sugars and the salt together. Drop in the butter and, with your fingers, rub and press the ingredients together until you've got moist crumbs. Add the vanilla and keep working the mixture with your hands until it holds its shape when you squeeze a handful. Pinch the topping into small morsels (you can do this in the same bowl you mixed everything in), cover and refrigerate for up to 2 days.

Preheat the oven to 350°. Place a 9-inch glass or ceramic pie plate on a parchment paper-lined baking sheet.

Make the filling: Put all of the filling ingredients in the pie plate and mix to combine. Using your hands, scatter with the topping, pressing it gently into the fruit mixture.

Bake for 45 to 55 minutes, or until the fruit is bubbling and the topping is golden brown. Transfer to a rack to cool to just warm or room temperature, and serve.

Lemon Curd

Lemon gives curd its appealing tang and tartness, but it's butter, and lots of it, that gives curd its voluptuous texture, its most memorable characteristic. If you'd like, you can grate some of the lemon zest into the curd—it's a nice touch. Packed into a canning jar, the curd makes a great gift; it'll keep in the fridge for about a month, ready to serve with ice cream, shortbread or toast.

1¼ cups sugar

¾ stick (6 tablespoons) unsalted butter, cut into pieces

1 large egg

6 large yolks

Freshly squeezed juice of 4 lemons (about ¾ cup)

makes 1½ cups

In a heavy-bottomed medium saucepan, combine all the ingredients and stir until the sugar is thoroughly moistened. Place the pan over medium-low heat, start stirring and don't stop until the butter melts, the curd thickens and you've got a gorgeous custard; plan on being on duty for minutes, give or take a couple of minutes. You'll know the curd is cooked when you dip a spoon into it, run your finger down the back of the spoon and the curd doesn't slip into the track you made. The curd may look thin, but it will thicken as it cools. Scrape the curd into a heatproof jar (or bowl), press a piece of plastic wrap against the surface and cool to room temperature. Once it's cooled, refrigerate until ready to use. The curd will keep, covered and refrigerated, for about a month.

Thank You!

hank you to the Short Stack team, Kaitlyn Goalen and Nick auchald, for inviting me to write about one of my favorite ingre-ients, and to Rotem Raffe for this edition's beautiful design— love this series! Hugs to the people whom I've been so lucky o have at my side for years: David Black, my agent; Jennifer lerrera, at the Black Agency; Mary Dodd, my recipe tester and ght hand for things cookbookery; and, of course, my husband nd fellow believer in the goodness of butter, Michael.

-Dorie Greenspan

hare your Short Stack cooking experiences with us
r just keep in touch) via:

 #shortstackeds facebook.com/shortstackeditions

@shortstackeds hello@shortstackeditions.com

Colophon

This edition of Short Stack was printed by Stephen Gould Corp. in Richmond, Virginia on Neenah Astrobrights Lunar Blue (interior) and Neenah Oxford White (cover) paper. The main text of the book is set in Futura and Jensen Pro, and the headlines are set in Lobster.

Available now at
ShortStackEditions.com:
